MEN IN THE MIDDLE

Marty Nabhan

BASKETBALL
HEROES

The Rourke Corporation, Inc.
Vero Beach, Florida 32964

The Rourke Corporation, Inc.
P.O. Box 3328, Vero Beach, FL 32964

Nabhan, Marty.
    Men in the middle / Marty Nabhan.
        p. cm. — (Basketball heroes)
    Includes bibliographical references and index.
    Summary: Discusses the role of the center in professional basketball and describes the play of some of the game's best, including Hakeem Olajuwon, Robert Parish, and Bill Laimbeer.
    ISBN 0-86593-158-5
    1. Basketball—United States—Offense—Juvenile literature. 2. Centers (Basketball)—United States—Biography—Juvenile literature. [1. Centers (Basketball) 2. Basketball.]
    I. Title. II. Series.
    GV889.N335   1992
796.357'0973—dc20   92-8760
                                                                                          CIP
                                                                                           AC

Series Editor: Gregory Lee
Editor: Marguerite Aronowitz
Book design and production: The Creative Spark, San Clemente, CA
Cover photograph: Damian Strohmeyer/ALLSPORT

Contents

The tip-off—where a basketball game begins and the centers go to work. Here rookie star Dikembe Mutombo (right) and Benoit Benjamin (left) square off.

Land Of The Giants

The players approach center court. Each man stands near a player from the other team. The referee in his black-and-white-striped shirt steps to the middle of the circle. He holds the ball at his waist, waiting to start the game. Then two giants come forward. The referee looks at them and tosses the ball skyward. The giants leap, each trying to outjump the other to tap the ball.

Every basketball game starts with a *tip-off*, when the ball is thrown into play. The team that controls the ball has the chance to score first. And the men in the middle are the first players to touch the ball.

Each NBA team has a big man in the middle. This man is often seven-feet tall—or even taller. He is called a *center*,

---

Center Trivia

Q: What center played more years in the NBA than any other player?
A: Kareem Abdul-Jabbar, with 20 seasons (1970-1989).

Q: Only two players in NBA history won Rookie of the Year and Most Valuable Player awards in the same year. Both were centers. Who were they?
A: Wilt Chamberlain, Philadelphia 76ers (1960), and Wes Unseld, Baltimore Bullets (1969).

Q: What player has more lifetime rebounds than any other?
A: Wilt Chamberlain, with 23,924.

because of the position he occupies on the court. The center usually stays close to the basket. If the other team misses a shot, the center is there to *rebound*, or grab the ball off the backboard. If a player from the other team tries to take a shot near the basket, the center is there to block it. Height has a lot to do with a center's reach.

Certain skills help a center play his position well. Because the area protected by a center is not as big as other players', a center does not have to be fast. He does not have to run great lengths in a hurry to do his job—but he does have to be quick. The best centers use quickness, leaping ability, strength, and intelligence to play their positions.

Quickness means the ability to cover short distances. A center has to be ready to keep his man from the basket. He also needs to react at a moment's notice if a man gets past the forwards or guards.

Leaping ability helps centers to block shots and get rebounds. It also helps them control the ball at the opening tip-off, or during other jump-ball situations.

Strength is especially important for centers. Although basketball is not a contact sport like football, a lot of pushing and shoving takes place under the basket as players try to get in position to shoot or rebound. A strong center can control his area and make it his own.

Timing is the ability to know when to do something. A skillful center knows precisely the right moment to jump for a rebound or for a *shot block*—batting the basketball away as an opponent shoots. A center also knows when to switch to defending another player.

Finally, a center needs to be intelligent. He needs to know and understand both the game of basketball and his position.

The modern NBA's first superstar was a center, big George Mikan of the Minneapolis Lakers. He led his team to five titles in their first six years.

In The Beginning

In the early days of basketball there were few outstanding big men. But as the modern NBA was organized, one thing became clear—big men won games.

A quick look at the first champions of the NBA shows that the Minneapolis Lakers (today the Los Angeles Lakers) won five of the first eight championships. Then the Boston Celtics came along and took 11 titles in the span of 13 years, including an incredible eight straight from 1959 to 1966. These two teams had one thing in common. They both had the most dominant big man of their day.

The Lakers boasted George Mikan, a six-foot, ten-inch monster in the middle. Mikan wore glasses, and looked a little like Clark Kent. But when the whistle blew and the game started, he played like Superman. Mikan bumped and banged in the middle and when the ball went to him, he was sure to score. No one could touch the Lakers when Mikan played, but by today's standards, he had one weakness: He was slow.

Still, in Mikan's day, the NBA did not have a 24-second clock. Now, once a team has the ball, they have only 24 seconds to shoot at the basket or the other team gets the ball. But Mikan's Lakers could take their time, let Mikan plod up and down the court, and shoot when they wanted to.

Mikan retired in his prime in 1954. Just a few years later, Bill Russell joined the Boston Celtics. The six-foot, nine-inch Russell has often been called one of the greatest centers who ever played the game. Russell brought agility and leaping ability to the position. He rarely scored a lot of points. His big contribution was in defense, blocked shots, and rebounds. Russell added intensity to any game, and his enthusiasm won games for the Celtics.

Russell once said, "I'd rather be what I am with a champion, than be the best scorer in the world with a team that never wins."

Perhaps Russell's comment was meant for Wilt "The Stilt" Chamberlain. For every person who says Russell was the greatest center, there are just as many who give the honor to the seven-foot, one-inch Chamberlain. Wilt exploded onto the scene in 1960 by averaging 37.6 points a game, and was named the

The awesome Wilt Chamberlain (13) is second in career points. In 14 seasons he threw in 31,419 points—an average of 30.1 per game that is still the all-time record.

The game's all-time leading scorer is Kareem Abdul-Jabbar, who played for 20 years and accumulated 38,387 points.

league's Rookie of the Year *and* Most Valuable Player. His next year he improved to 38.4 points. But imagine the league's reaction during Chamberlain's third season, when he averaged 50.4 points per game!

Throughout the 1960s, Russell and Chamberlain battled it out. Russell, backed by a better team, usually came away victorious. Then in the 1970s, a new kid came along named Lew Alcindor.

Alcindor, the seven-foot, two-inch star out of the University of California, Los Angeles (UCLA), became an instant star. In just his second professional year he led the Milwaukee Bucks to a victory in the NBA finals. He changed his name to Kareem Abdul-Jabbar, and enjoyed many years of greatness in the pros, spending the majority of his career with the Los Angeles Lakers. He was already a 10-year veteran when rookie Magic Johnson joined the Lakers, and the pair ushered in a new era of greatness nicknamed "Showtime." Showtime featured a fast break run by Johnson and the trademark skyhook of Abdul-Jabbar.

By the time he retired, Abdul-Jabbar had played 20 years, played for six NBA championship teams, was named league MVP six times, and scored more points than anybody in the history of pro basketball.

Today's Center

The 1950s, 1960s, and 1970s were dominated by the men in the middle. The center was the most important man on the court. Teams needed good, powerful centers in order to be successful.

In the 1980s, however, things changed. Earvin "Magic" Johnson, the six-foot, nine-inch guard of the Los Angeles Lakers, showed that a big man could have moves, dribble the ball, and run the offense. Throughout the decade, players got taller, quicker, and stronger. Now the emphasis has shifted from centers to guards as the dominant players on a team.

In the 1990s the three best centers in today's game—Hakeem Olajuwon of the Houston Rockets, Patrick Ewing of the New York Knicks, and David Robinson of the San Antonio Spurs—have never won an NBA Championship. All three of these centers and their teams lost early in the 1991 playoffs. Who went to the NBA Finals? The teams with the two best guards in the game: the Chicago Bulls with Michael Jordan, and the Lakers with Magic Johnson.

In today's game players are bigger, faster, and stronger than they have ever been. Everyone seems more athletic and capable than ever. Some teams, like the Golden State Warriors, enjoy success by playing as many as four quick guards at a time, with no real center in the middle.

In recent years teams have won without an intimidating center. The Detroit Pistons won back-to-back championships in 1989 and 1990 without a top-notch center. The Chicago Bulls did the same in 1991. They did it instead with quickness and defense. No longer were smaller players feeding the ball to their big man in the key. Having a dominant center doesn't guarantee that a team will beat everyone. But many team owners and coaches still believe it is important to get a big man and build the team around him.

Every year in the NBA teams get a chance to pick the best players from college basketball. This is known as the NBA *draft*. In the draft, teams with the most losses during the previous season have the first picks. In the 1980s, teams with the first selection in the draft chose centers seven out of ten times.

Guard Michael Jordan is considered the best player in the game. Yet in 1984, he wasn't even the top draft choice. Jordan was selected third, behind two centers: Olajuwon and Sam Bowie, now of the New Jersey Nets.

The desire to pick centers shows that people are still hoping for a big man to dominate the game. History is on their side. Hall of Fame guard Oscar Robertson needed Abdul-Jabbar to finally reach the NBA Finals. Guard Jerry West needed Wilt Chamberlain, center Bill Walton led the Portland Trail Blazers to a championship, and Magic Johnson never won a championship after Abdul-Jabbar retired.

The Dream

In 1981, the Houston Rockets were tough. With center Moses Malone, they went all the way to the NBA Championship. There, they lost to the Boston Celtics, four games to one. Things went downhill for the Rockets after that. The very next year, they only won 14 games. The year after, they managed 29 victories, while losing 53. Moses Malone went to the Philadelphia 76ers where he helped them win an NBA Championship in 1983. But the Rockets went nowhere.

The Rockets tried to rebuild their team. In 1983 they got the first choice of all college players and chose seven-foot, four-inch Ralph Sampson. Despite a great rookie season from Sampson, it wasn't enough. But the dream really began when the Rockets made Hakeem Olajuwon their first draft pick in 1984. The Rockets hoped he would lead them back to the playoffs.

Olajuwon grew up in the African city of Lagos, Nigeria. Although he was tall, he did not play much basketball as a boy. In Nigeria the big sport is soccer, and Olajuwon was a goalie for his team.

"I had fights all the time," Olajuwon said. "I was too tall, too thin. They were picking on me because I was too abnormal." An American basketball coach, Chris Pond, saw Olajuwon's ability and thought he would be a good player. He arranged for Olajuwon to visit some colleges in the United States. Olajuwon picked Houston because the weather was warm, like in Nigeria. The University of Houston was happy about that. Little by little, Olajuwon learned the game of basketball. With every contest, he got better. Soon, his knowledge of basketball caught up with his tremendous ability. Olajuwon led Houston to the National College Athletic Association (NCAA) championship.

Hakeem "The Dream" Olajuwon was a wanted man. Many teams in the NBA needed a big man like him. Only one team got the chance. The local Houston team made Olajuwon their number one pick. With Olajuwon, the Rockets now had two big men. Ralph Sampson was moved to forward, and Olajuwon became

Hakeem Olajuwon is one of today's best centers, frequently leading his position in rebounds and blocked shots, as well as averaging more than 20 points per game.

the man in the middle. The duo was known as "the twin towers." Other teams feared Houston. The Rockets could score just about whenever they wanted. The object was simply to get the ball in the hands of one of their big men. The big men would do the rest.

But it was on defense where Olajuwon shined. He could block the other teams' shots with power. Shorter players thought twice about driving to the basket. In the back of their minds, they saw Hakeem waiting to sail into the air to reject their shots.

That very year, the Rockets became contenders. They made the playoffs after winning 48 games. In the 1985-86 season, things got even better. The Rockets went all the way to the NBA Finals before losing to the Boston Celtics. Many successful seasons followed. Although Houston didn't make the Finals again in the 1980s, Olajuwon continued to dominate the game. He is the league's leading active rebounder, averaging 12.6 rebounds per game.

"*Olajuwon* means being on top," Olajuwon once explained. "And *Hakeem* is Arabic for a wise man, a doctor." As for being on top, Olajuwon knows how to do that. In his 10 seasons of basketball for the University of Houston and the Houston Rockets, he has never had a losing season.

"I think a lot of people don't understand how much I want to win," he said. "They don't know what I would give to get a championship."

For Olajuwon it may take a strong prescription to win it all in the NBA. But until then, Olajuwon continues to be the most dominant big man in the game today.

The Boston Celtics would not have won nine out of ten championships in the 1960s without Bill Russell, one of the game's greatest centers.

Dominating The Paint

There is a special area on the basketball court that's so important, it is known by many names: the lane, the key, the middle, the inside. It starts at the free-throw line and ends at the base line underneath the backboard. It is 19 feet long and 16 feet wide. It is so important that it is a different color from the rest of the floor, which gives it another name: the paint.

The paint is the center's territory. If an opponent enters it to shoot, the center is there to challenge him. Centers must be quick to protect the paint.

Of course, in the NBA teams play *man-to-man defense*. That means that each player is responsible for guarding one man on the other team. Guarding an area instead of a player is called *illegal defense*. But if an offensive player beats his man to the paint, it is up to the center to quickly switch from guarding his own man to stopping the new intruder.

In the early days of basketball, the lane was only six feet wide. But players like George Mikan were so good at guarding in the lane that the area was widened. The wider area made it tougher for the center to be everywhere at once. But ball handlers who drove the lane still knew they would be facing a big man in the middle.

"To be a great shooter, you must be able to

concentrate," said former NBA center Ed Macauley. "When you go up for a shot, there can be only one thing on your mind—the hoop. That's where Bill Russell changed things. Now you had two things to concentrate on: the hoop and 'Where is he?' You'd have to stop for just a split-second to see where he was. And in that split-second, one of his teammates would catch up to you. Russell's biggest asset was that element of distraction."

Crafty teams try to draw the center out of the paint. They play their big man at the top of the key, forcing the defensive center to come out and guard him. The quickest centers adapt. They guard their man outside, and as soon as the ball goes toward the lane they drop back and plug up the middle.

The mark of a good center is his ability to play defense and intimidate the other team. And that means they must be good shot blockers and rebounders.

Shot Blocking

A quick guard dribbles while keeping an eye on the 24-second clock. As the seconds tick away, he spots an opening. He dribbles into the clear. He stops in an instant, jumps, and releases the ball for an easy shot. But as the ball floats effortlessly toward the basket, a hand comes from nowhere, knocking it away like a fly-swatter.

In basketball's early days, a ball that left a player's hands was fair game, no matter where it was. It could be blocked on its way up or its way down. There weren't many players tall enough to block a ball on its way down. Then along came Mikan and a seven-footer named Bob Kurland of the Phillips Oilers. They blocked so many shots, the rule was changed. Blocking a shot on its downward path, or *goaltending*, was not allowed. If goaltending was called, it was an automatic two points for the shooting team.

To avoid the goaltending call, shot blocking became a skill of reflexes, timing, and quickness. A player had to jump just right to block his opponent's shots. If he is really skillful, he has enough control to tap the ball to a teammate or to himself, instead of just knocking it out of bounds.

Shot blocking statistics weren't kept when Russell and Chamberlain played professional basketball. In the modern game, those statistics are very important. They show how often the big men prevent teams from scoring.

Today's Big Three—Olajuwon, Robinson, and Ewing—are all expert shot-blockers. But that is just one part of their overall game. Some players specialize in blocking shots. Indeed, it is the main reason they are on the court.

Mark Eaton of the Utah Jazz almost didn't play basketball in college. Eaton was working at a garage when a California junior college coach spotted him. Actually, it was hard to miss Eaton—he stands seven-feet, four-inches and weighs 290 pounds. Eaton went on to play center for UCLA. He wasn't a star in college, but the Jazz drafted him anyway. "We took him because you can't coach height," said Utah coach Frank Layden. In other words, you can't teach a player to be tall.

Eaton worked hard and became an imposing force in the middle. The paint was Eaton's domain, and few players dared to trespass. And when they did, they often changed their shot, expecting Eaton to appear. In the 1984-85 season, Eaton did more than change shots. He blocked 456 of them, averaging 5.6 blocks per game. That still stands as an NBA record.

If Eaton's presence is frightening on the basketball court, imagine what opponents must think when the long arm of Manute Bol approaches them. Wherever Bol travels in the NBA he is the tallest man on the court. At

Mark Eaton (53) has been one of Utah's mainstays for a decade. He routinely blocks 200 shots a season, and his career shooting percentage is .650.

seven-feet, seven-inches, he presents quite an obstacle to anyone trying to make a point. He is not strong; he is not agile. He is there for one purpose alone: to block shots.

Bol came from Sudan, Africa, where he is said to have once speared a lion. Since joining the NBA, Bol has averaged almost four blocked shots per game over his career.

Being seven-feet, seven-inches has its drawbacks off the court, however. Clothes have to be specially made for him. Bol's long legs make car travel difficult. His house was built with eight-foot doors on the inside, so that he doesn't have to duck when walking through them. But on the court, his height only gets in the way of the other team.

"I am never bothered by the fact that I am tall," Bol said. "When I was younger I was bothered, but not now. My height is a gift from God. That is what I say. Who knows what God may be dreaming of for us? There is a reason. Look at what he has dreamed of for me."

Rebounding

When a shot goes up, players circle around the basket. All eyes watch as the ball spins toward the hoop. Sometimes the ball does not go through. Instead, it hits the rim and bounces against the backboard. As it comes back down to the court, players fight for possession. Whichever team gets the ball will be the team to get the next chance to score.

Catching the ball after it has hit the basket or backboard following a shot is known as rebounding. Rebounding is a key skill for the men in the middle.

Russell and Chamberlain were masters at rebounding. They each have more than 20,000 career rebounds to their credit. Another tough rebounder in his day was Wes Unseld of the Baltimore Bullets (now a head coach in the NBA). Although Unseld was the shortest center in the league (just six-feet, seven-inches), he was strong and stocky. He could get good position, even against bigger men.

Rebounding is more that just height and leaping ability. It takes practice to know and anticipate how the ball will bounce. Is there spin on the ball? Was it a long shot? What direction did the shot come from? Where did it hit the rim or backboard? All these factors determine where the ball will go next.

More important than height, leaping ability, and anticipation, however, is position. The expert rebounder knows how to put himself between his opponent and the

No one towers over his opponents quite like Manute Bol, the 76ers'
big man.

basket. Size and strength help, along with good old-fashioned pushing and shoving. The struggle for rebounds or "boards" can be true battles.

Smart players combine all their skills to get the ball back. That wisdom often comes with time. Many centers have been in the league for ten or more years. This experience gives them an edge over the younger players.

Robert Parish of the Boston Celtics is an example of one such player. Parish has always been a steady performer. In the 1980s, he went to four championships, helping the Celtics win three of them. But he seems to get better with age. After 15 seasons in the NBA, the "Chief" is still one of basketball's hardest workers. He has a nose for the basketball, and always seems to be around to tip the ball in, grab it from an opponent, or pass it to an open teammate.

While Parish is the oldest active player in the NBA, Moses Malone of the Milwaukee Bucks has more years in the league. The six-foot, ten-inch Malone didn't play college basketball. He had so much talent at an early age, he was able to go from high school basketball straight to the pros. Throughout his career Malone has been a winner. He led the Houston Rockets to the NBA Finals in 1981, and helped star forward Julius Erving win a championship ring with the Philadelphia 76ers. He has slowed down over the years, but is still a power under the basket. He has more points and rebounds than any active player, and his more than 8,000 free throws surpass anyone who ever played the game.

A veteran center who relies more on experience than physical ability is six-foot, eleven-inch Bill Laimbeer of the Detroit Pistons. He slams and bangs with the best. His rough tactics have been called dirty by some, but Laimbeer is proud of them. Those who play against

One of the elder statesmen in the NBA is Robert Parish of the Boston Celtics, a nine-time All-Star with a .720 shooting percentage.

Laimbeer sometimes get so angry that they forget to play good basketball, and that can lose games. Laimbeer is also the best outside-shooting center in the game.

Veteran James Edwards of the Los Angeles Clippers adds a different spark to the game. Edwards comes off the bench to give the scoring a boost. His turnaround jump shot is almost unstoppable. It's hard to block a big man's shot. Edwards makes it harder by starting with his back to the basket. He spins and jumps backwards while shooting. The result is usually two points.

Centers create obstacles for the other team. They fill the lane, and challenge anyone who enters the painted area. Defense is the name of the game, and centers are in the middle of the action. But as we shall see, there are other ways for these giants to dominate a basketball court.

The Franchise

On May 12, 1985, seven teams crossed their fingers. They were hoping for good luck. In past years, the team with the worst record in basketball got the first pick in the college draft. In 1985, the seven teams that didn't get to the playoffs had their team name and logo placed on a card. The cards were put in envelopes and mixed up in a drum. One by one the envelopes were picked. And one lucky team would be chosen to pick the first draft choice.

The team would be lucky because in 1985 there was a special player in the draft. His name was Patrick Ewing. Each of the seven teams wanted a chance to pick him. Coaches thought they could build a team around him. He was the type of player who was called a "franchise." In other words, surround him with anyone and the team would be a contender.

Like Olajuwon, Ewing didn't grow up playing basketball. He was a goalie for his soccer team on the Caribbean island of Jamaica. In 1975, Ewing and his family moved to the Boston area, where he traded in his soccer ball for a basketball.

By the time he was in high school, college coaches took notice. When Georgetown coach John Thompson saw Ewing play, he said, "With that kid, we'll win the national championship." Thompson knew what he was talking about. With Ewing at center, Georgetown went to the championship three out of four years, winning it all in 1984.

Ewing was an incredible defensive player. He dominated the paint, and it became a "no-man's land." Another college coach remarked, "Patrick Ewing is the

Patrick Ewing is one of the league's swiftest centers, and he often powers through the lane with some monster stuffs.

best player ever to play college basketball." There were plenty who agreed.

The envelopes were pulled from the drum placing them in draft order, and one by one they were opened. Starting with the seventh envelope, an NBA official read them aloud. One by one the teams saw their hopes fade. When it was narrowed down to the top two, the Indiana Pacers and the New York Knicks crossed their fingers. The Indiana Pacers were number two. The Knicks were joyous; they knew they had won.

But the NBA today is not the NBA of 20, or even 10 years ago. A team needs more than one great player to be a winner. For two more seasons, the Knicks lost more games than they won. Although their new center was fun to watch, the fans became restless. The team didn't seem to get better, but Ewing did.

In college, Ewing was always feared for his defense. In the pros he worked on his scoring. In 1991, he had a scoring average of 26.6 points per game, fifth highest in the league and higher than any other center. By then the Knicks had made the playoffs four years in a row. And although they still hadn't won the NBA championship, one thing was clear: Ewing was once again at the top of his class.

Every fan loves to see a slam dunk—especially when it is done with such style, as the Spurs' David Robinson demonstrates.

Scoring Up Close

The center sees his team's point guard with the ball. As the guard dribbles, the center moves near the lane with his back to the basket. An opponent leans against him, pushing for position. The center raises his arm, showing the guard he's ready. The guard tosses the ball to the center. The center bounces the ball as his opponent continues to lean against him. The center spins, pivoting on one foot, and gets around his opponent. He leaves the ground, hovering toward the basket. With no one there to block it, he slams the ball through the hoop for an easy score.

There are good shots and there are bad shots in basketball. Scoring is done by getting the best shot. Usually, the closer you get to the basket, the better the

Center Trivia

Q: *What are the most points scored by a player in any one game in NBA history?*
A: *Wilt Chamberlain of the Philadelphia 76ers scored 100 points against the New York Knicks on March 2, 1962. In that game he also set records for most field goals (36) and most free throws (28).*

Q: *What center has won the Most Valuable Player award more than any other player?*
A: *Kareem Abdul-Jabbar won the honor of MVP in 1971 and 1972 when he played for the Milwaukee Bucks and in 1974, 1976, 1977, and 1980 when he played for the Los Angeles Lakers.*

shot. Since the center is the closest man to the basket, he has a lot of good shots.

The Arsenal

Centers have an arsenal of shots from which to choose. Each center has his specialty, according to his strengths and abilities.

The *slam dunk* is perhaps the most sure shot in basketball. The player goes up hard and pushes the ball through the hoop. It is also called the jam or the "stuff shot."

The slam dunk is such a sure thing that it was banned from college basketball during the years Lew Alcindor (Abdul-Jabbar) played. The NCAA was afraid that, with the jam, Alcindor and UCLA would be unstoppable. After Alcindor graduated, the slam dunk was brought back to college ball.

Another drawback of the slam dunk appeared in the 1970s and 1980s. Some players were so powerful when they dunked, they shattered the backboard glass. Breakaway rims were made, so they could absorb the pressure of a player hanging on them. They are designed to give, almost like shock absorbers on a car.

The slam dunk is a popular shot in basketball. Many years ago, only a few players could make the shot. Now almost every player in the NBA can stuff the ball through the hoop. People enjoy seeing good slams so much that a slam dunk contest has been made a regular part of the mid-season NBA All-Star Game.

Hook Shots

The *hook* is another good short-range shot. The shooter swings the ball overhead in a sweeping motion, using the hand farthest from the basket. It is a high-arcing shot that is very difficult to block. Kareem Abdul-Jabbar used his version of this shot—the "sky hook"—to

*Kareem Abdul-Jabbar's patented skyhook was his favorite shot,
where he could use his height to avoid blocked shots.*

score many of his NBA-record 38,387 points.

Another hard shot to block is the fallaway or *fadeaway shot*. It is really a jump shot during which a player jumps backward, away from the basket, in order to keep the shot from being blocked.

Being so close to the basket, big men sometimes make simple *lay-ups* or lay-ins. A lay-up is a shot taken right next to the basket that either banks off the backboard or goes right in. One type of lay-in is called a finger roll. This is a shot taken with your hand near the rim, letting the ball roll off your fingers into the basket.

If a center shoots near the basket, he has to do it quickly. An offensive player can only be in the painted area for three seconds at a time. If he is there longer, the referee can call a three-second violation, and the other team will get the ball.

Some big men like to shoot from a little farther out. Sam Bowie of the New Jersey Nets, Bill Laimbeer of the Pistons, Brad Daugherty of the Cleveland Cavaliers, and Vlade Divac of the Los Angeles Lakers often shoot from ten feet or farther.

Other Offensive Weapons

The men in the middle do more on offense than score. Often, they help their teammates to score. Because centers are hard to stop, teams sometimes guard the center with two men. This is called *double-teaming*. When a center is double-teamed, he can look and find an open teammate. If a center's pass leads directly to a teammate scoring, the center gets an *assist*. Brad Daugherty of the Cleveland Cavaliers and Sam Bowie of the New Jersey Nets are two centers who often get assists.

Centers also help the offense by setting *screens*. To set a screen, a center stands by a man guarding his teammate. When his teammate dribbles by, the center's

From this position, Benoit Benjamin can set a pick or screen for a teammate, or post up if he gets a pass.

body blocks the opponent, freeing his teammate for an open shot. As centers are usually the biggest men on the court, they can set some big screens.

One of the most important ways a man in the middle can help his team's offense is by getting offensive rebounds. If his teammate misses a shot, the center can keep the ball alive by getting the rebound and taking another shot. Teams that get the most offensive rebounds get two, three, four or more shots at a time.

Some centers have developed the ability to tip in a missed shot. By timing his jump, the center doesn't have to catch the rebound and bring it down. With one big hand, he can tap the ball gently into the basket. Or he can grab it in mid-air and slam it through the hoop.

However a center helps his team—whether in rebounds or blocks, dunks or assists— one thing is certain: In a game of big men, they rise above all the others.

The Admiral

In 1987, the San Antonio Spurs were facing a dilemma. The team was horrible, but they had the number one pick in

Kevin Duckworth is the Portland Trail Blazer's man in the middle.

the college draft. So far so good. The best college player was without a doubt the Navy's David Robinson. The Spurs knew Robinson could be the answer to their problems. But there was a catch. Robinson owed two years to the Navy in their civil engineering corps. That meant that if the Spurs picked Robinson, he wouldn't be able to join the team until the 1989 season.

So did they pick another player that could help them immediately, or wait two years for Robinson? For the Spurs the choice was easy. They picked Robinson and suffered through two more losing seasons.

Actually, the Spurs were lucky. Robinson originally had a five-year commitment to the Navy to be a line officer. But he kept growing. And growing. He grew six inches from the time he entered the Naval Academy. At seven-feet, one-inch, he had outgrown most of the planes, ships, and submarines. Navy Secretary John Lehman ruled that Robinson was too tall to qualify as a line officer.

"I never dreamed of being a pro in any sport," Robinson said. "I knew a lot try out, a lot don't make it. I was a pretty practical kid."

And tall. Let's not forget tall. As a senior in high school, Robinson was six-feet, seven-inches, but had never played basketball. His high school coach changed that. Robinson had a great senior year, and colleges stood in line to recruit him.

Still, Robinson wasn't serious about his game. His goal was to get an engineering degree, and he had his sights set on the U.S. Naval Academy. For the Navy team, Robinson had his ups and downs. But by the time he reached his top height and ability, it was clear. Robinson's future would be in basketball.

After serving his stint in the Navy, Robinson came on board with the Spurs. In no time the Spurs were sailing for unchartered waters: the playoffs.

Stretching before a game is San Antonio's favorite center: David Robinson.

The season before his arrival, the Spurs had 21 wins and 61 losses. In his rookie year, Robinson turned it all around. The Spurs won 56 games with Robinson at the helm. The 35-game improvement was the biggest single-season turnaround in NBA history. He earned the nickname, "the Admiral." Robinson made the All-Star team and was named Rookie of the Year.

And he was just getting started.

About his second year, ex-Spurs Coach Larry Brown said, "Robinson has gotten better so quickly. He has improved everywhere. He has elevated his whole game. His focus was better than his first year."

In 1991, Robinson was first in the league in rebounding, averaging 13 per game. He was second in blocked shots with 3.9 per game. He was ninth in scoring and shooting percentage. And he led the Spurs to their second straight Midwest Division title. According to expert analyst Dick Vitale, "Robinson's combination of size, strength, speed, and quickness is unmatched."

Not only is he a great player. Robinson is also a good role model. He is involved with community and national charities. He gives his time and money freely. For Spurs' home games, he buys 50 tickets for the upper level and donates them to San Antonio schools. The tickets are given to kids selected by their teachers for their good grades and citizenship. The section in which they sit is called "Mr. Robinson's Neighborhood."

"I consider myself to be like the average guy," Robinson said. "The only thing I think about is being the best person I can be. I try to let the kids see that. I have a God-given talent. I try to keep a close base on who I am. That's what is important."

And for the Spurs, who knows? Maybe one of these seasons their ship will finally come in. If it does, the Admiral will be ready.

The Cleveland Cavaliers are happy they drafted Brad Daugherty—a center who does many things well, from passing to assisting to rebounding.

Rising To The Top

Centers Olajuwon, Ewing, and Robinson have different skills, and each can dominate a game. Olajuwon's quickness, Ewing's strength, and Robinson's athletic ability are hard to match. Nevertheless, there are several young players who are fighting to make their mark in the league. Many of them are earning the respect of their opponents, and may be ready to join the Elite Three.

Brad Daugherty of the Cleveland Cavaliers has had some injuries, but still plays great basketball at center. Noted NBA expert Pete Newell said, "When healthy, Daugherty can score on anybody in the league. He can pass the ball better than the other three [Olajuwon, Ewing, and Robinson] and has just as much mobility."

Daugherty is a smooth offensive player, scoring with finesse and agility. His only weakness is shot blocking, but his game has made Cleveland a contender.

Another up-and-coming center is six-feet, eleven-inch Rony Seikaly of the Miami Heat. Seikaly works hard, and has consistently improved his game. He has a variety of shots that makes him dangerous. Players double-team Seikaly when he gets near the basket. If he can continue to get better, more and more people will notice both him and the Heat.

Seven-footer Benoit Benjamin of the Seattle Supersonics has been criticized at times for being lazy.

Tough rebounder Rony Seikaly is part of the Miami Heat's fast rise from expansion team to playoff contender.

But when Benjamin comes to play, he is absolutely unstoppable. Rik Smits has the physical skills to make an impact with the Indiana Pacers. At seven-feet, four-inches he gives opposing teams headaches with his hustle and solid play. Injuries and lack of quickness have slowed him, but he's still young enough to improve. Olden Polynice of the Los Angeles Clippers has the quickness, jumping ability, and enthusiasm to go far. With a few great years, he and Benjamin and Smits could be at the top of the league.

Perhaps no center improved as much in his second year as Vlade Divac of the Lakers. Divac's strength is in ball handling and outside shooting. Divac came from Yugoslavia and is used to the less physical style of European basketball. Although he gets banged around by stronger, heavier players, Divac still manages amazing offensive moves. When the Lakers made the playoffs in 1991, Divac came alive. He played Olajuwon to a standstill. And in the Finals, he showed the abilities of a superstar. Sidelined with a back injury for much of his third NBA season, Divac may have trouble fighting back to form. But if he does, look for him to be one of the strongest centers in the West.

Although Denver Nuggets' rookie Dikembe Mutombo has only played a short while, his statistics were solid. This seven-foot, two-inch center showed potential on both defense and offense that should enable him to go a long way.

A native of Zaire, Africa, Mutombo has adapted well to the United States. He earned a degree in linguistics at Georgetown. He speaks French, English, Spanish, Portuguese, and five African dialects. Mutombo believes in keeping his body healthy and works hard to play well. With his intelligence and abilities, he might be alongside the "Big Three" before too long—after he gets used to NBA play.

One of the center's jobs is to defend his basket and fight for rebounds, as demonstrated here by up-and-coming Laker big man Vlade Divac.

Mutombo was the fourth person taken in the college draft in 1991. After his success with the Nuggets, an NBA official said, "If the draft were held again, Mutombo would be the first player taken."

Many teams are already looking ahead to the college drafts for future NBA centers. Although it is still too early to tell if these players will make an impact, their size and abilities are getting the pro scouts excited.

Most coaches believe that Shaquille O'Neal of Louisiana State University could play in the pros today. Even though he's only 20 years old, he has been compared to Ewing, Olajuwon, Robinson, and even Bill Russell when they were in college.

"He's like Wilt Chamberlain reincarnated," said Wilt the Stilt himself. "That's the closest thing to myself I've seen in college basketball."

"The thing that stands out," said Phoenix Suns assistant coach Lionel Hollins, "is his agility and mobility for a guy his size. Olajuwon would be his closest competitor."

"He's definitely a player everyone wants," said Laker general manager Jerry West. "The thing I like most about him is that he's got a great attitude on the court. He's willing to learn and improve his game."

Shawn Bradley is one of the most noticeable players in college basketball. The seven-foot, six-inch freshman of Brigham Young University shows great agility in spite of his height. But it is his defense that gets the praise. He blocked 10 shots in one game during the NCAA tournament in 1991, tying a college record.

As the game of professional basketball heads for the year 2000, perhaps centers will become so tall and agile that the NBA will have to raise the height of the basket, just to keep the game fair. With great men in the middle, there seems to be no limit to the heights this exciting game can reach.

Stats

Most Valuable Players: Centers*		
Year	**Player**	**Pts.**
1958	Bill Russell, Boston	16.6
1960	Wilt Chamberlain, Philadelphia	37.6
1961	Bill Russell, Boston	16.9
1962	Bill Russell, Boston	18.9
1963	Bill Russell, Boston	16.8
1965	Bill Russell, Boston	14.1
1966	Wilt Chamberlain, Philadelphia	33.5
1967	Wilt Chamberlain, Philadelphia	24.1
1968	Wilt Chamberlain, Philadelphia	24.3
1969	Wes Unseld, Baltimore	13.8
1970	Willis Reed, New York	21.7
1971	Lew Alcindor, Milwaukee	31.7
1972	Kareem Abdul-Jabbar, Milwaukee	34.8
1973	Dave Cowens, Boston	20.5
1974	Kareem Abdul-Jabbar, Los Angeles	27.0
1976	Kareem Abdul-Jabbar, Los Angeles	27.7
1977	Kareem Abdul-Jabbar, Los Angeles	26.2
1978	Bill Walton, Portland	18.9
1979	Moses Malone, Houston	24.8
1980	Kareem Abdul-Jabbar, Los Angeles	24.8
1982	Moses Malone, Houston	31.1
1983	Moses Malone, Philadelphia	24.5

* Winners of the Podoloff Trophy for regular season play since 1956.

Glossary

ASSIST. A pass that results directly in a basket.

BALL HANDLER. The player who has control of the basketball.

BASE LINE. The line underneath the backboard.

BOX OUT. Putting your body between your opponent and the basket, establishing your position under the backboard and preventing an opponent from intruding on it.

CENTER. Usually the team's tallest player who patrols the area near the basket both on offense and defense.

DEFENSE. Guarding the team that has the ball. The defense tries to keep the offense from scoring.

DOUBLE-TEAMING. Using two defensive players to cover one offensive player.

DUNK. To slam or drop the ball into the basket from above the rim.

FADEAWAY. A jump shot during which a player leaps backward, away from the basket, in order to avoid having the shot blocked.

FREE-THROW LANE. Also known as the *key*. It is a 19-foot by 16-foot rectangle around the basket, and the best shooting area.

GOALTENDING. Interfering with a shot on its downward arc to the basket, or interfering with a ball that is rolling on the rim of the basket.

HOOK SHOT or SKY HOOK. A high-arcing shot usually taken by a center.

LAY-UP or LAY-IN. A shot usually banked off the backboard from the side of the basket or from the front of the basket.

MAN-TO-MAN DEFENSE. When each defensive player is assigned a specific offensive player to cover, no matter where that player goes on the court.

OFFENSE. The team that has the ball in its possession.

OPEN MAN. A player without the ball who is in a good position to shoot.

PAINT. The *lane* or the *key*.

REBOUND. To grab the ball off either the offensive backboard or the defensive backboard.

SCREEN. An offensive player establishing his position in front of a defensive player, enabling a teammate to use him as a screen in getting free for a shot or a drive to the basket.

SHOT BLOCKING. When a defensive player jumps between the ball and basket to deflect a shot.

TIP-OFF. The start of the game when the referee tosses the basketball in the air. Each team's center tries to tip the ball to his own teammate.

Bibliography

Aaseng, Nate. *Basketball: You Are The Coach*. Minneapolis: Lerner Publications, 1983.

Aaseng, Nate. *Basketball's High Flyers*. Minneapolis: Lerner Publications, 1980.

Anderson, Dave. *The Story of Basketball*. New York: William Morrow, 1988.

Editors of *Sports Illustrated. Sports Illustrated Basketball*. New York: J.B. Lippincott, 1971.

Finney, Shan. *Basketball*. New York: Franklin Watts, 1982.

Hirschberg, Al. *Basketball's Greatest Stars*. New York: G.P. Putnam's Sons, 1963.

Liss, Howard. *Basketball Talk For Beginners*. New York: Julian Messner, 1970.

Meserole, Mike, ed. *The 1992 Information Please Sports Almanac*. Boston: Houghton Mifflin.

Olney, Ross. *Basketball*. Racine, Wisconsin: Western Publishing, 1975.

Ostler, Scott and Steve Springer. *Winnin' Times*. New York: Macmillan Publishing, 1988.

Rainbolt, Richard. *Basketball's Big Men*. Minneapolis: Lerner Publications, 1975.

Riley, Pat. *Showtime*. New York: Warner Books, 1988.

Ryan, Bob. *The Boston Celtics*. New York: Addison-Wesley, 1989.

Siegener, Ray, ed. *The Basketball Skill Book*. New York: Atheneum, 1974.

Sullivan, George. *Winning Basketball*. New York: David McKay, 1976.

Picture Credits

Index